English Workbook

AGE 9–11

Spelling and Vocabulary

Susan Elkin

GALORE PARK

AN HACHETTE UK COMPANY

About the author

Susan Elkin is an award-winning journalist who has taught English in five different secondary schools, both independent and state, over many years, most recently at Benenden. She is the author of over 30 books including *English Year 9* and the *English A* Study Guide* and has been a regular contributor to many newspapers and magazines including the *Daily Telegraph* and *Daily Mail*. She is Education Editor at *The Stage* and writes blogs for *The Independent*. You can read about Susan's early classroom experiences in her 2013 ebook *Please Miss We're Boys*.

Every effort has been made to trace all copyright holders, but if any have been inadvertently overlooked the publishers will be pleased to make the necessary arrangements at the first opportunity.

Although every effort has been made to ensure that website addresses are correct at time of going to press, Galore Park cannot be held responsible for the content of any website mentioned in this book. It is sometimes possible to find a relocated web page by typing in the address of the home page for a website in the URL window of your browser.

Hachette UK's policy is to use papers that are natural, renewable and recyclable products and made from wood grown in sustainable forests. The logging and manufacturing processes are expected to conform to the environmental regulations of the country of origin.

Orders: please contact Bookpoint Ltd, 130 Milton Park, Abingdon, Oxon OX14 4SB. Telephone: +44 (0)1235 827827. Lines are open 9.00a.m.–5.00p.m., Monday to Saturday, with a 24-hour message answering service. Visit our website at www.galorepark.co.uk for details of other revision guides for Common Entrance, examination papers and Galore Park publications.

Published by Galore Park Publishing Ltd
An Hachette UK company
338 Euston Road, London, NW1 3BH
www.galorepark.co.uk

Text copyright © Susan Elkin Ltd 2014
The right of Susan Elkin to be identified as the author of this Work has been asserted by her in accordance with sections 77 and 78 of the Copyright, Designs and Patents Act 1988.

Impression number 10 9 8 7 6 5 4 3 2 1
                  2018 2017 2016 2015 2014

Typeset in India
Printed in Spain

A catalogue record for this title is available from the British Library.

ISBN: 978 1 471829 64 2

Contents

Have a dictionary handy as you work through this book, to check your spellings and look up definitions.

Introduction

Words are wonderful. And English has more words than any other European language, which is why we so often have several words very similar in meaning. That's what makes it such an exciting language to use, study and play with.

To make the best use of this marvellous language of ours, however, you need to know exactly what words mean, how they have come to mean what they do and, of course, how to spell them correctly.

This workbook will help 9–11 year olds to improve their skills in:

● understanding what words mean
● using newly learned words confidently and accurately
● recognising links between words as a way of both understanding and spelling them
● spelling both everyday words and less familiar ones as they are added to personal vocabulary
● enjoying words and their quirks
● working out how words have acquired their meanings over time
● using spelling rules where they can be applied
● perfecting the spelling of words that apparently defy all logic!

Although this book is not linked to a particular examination syllabus, it will help users prepare for:

● Common Entrance 11+ in English
● 11+ entry English tests set by individual independent schools
● 11+ in English for selective state-funded schools in certain local authorities (such as Kent)
● National Curriculum Key Stage 2 SATS English tests
● pre-tests.

You will also find it useful if you are involved in homeschooling because every activity is fully explained and self-contained.

Answers are supplied in a pull-out section in the middle of the book. Sometimes – in the case of spellings, for example – these are the only acceptable response. In many cases though, the child needs to apply imagination and ingenuity and supply his or her own. Mine are often just suggestions or examples to point the way.

Susan Elkin, September 2014

-os or -oes?

Nouns ending in **o** *usually* end **-os** when they are plural.

> For example, words that:
>
> - come from Spanish or Italian or are to do with music (ponchos, patios, sopranos)
> - end in a double vowel (tattoos, radios)
> - are abbreviations (hippos, photos).

But there are a number of exceptions that end **-oes**:

> buffaloes, calicoes, dingoes, dominoes, echoes, embargoes, heroes, jingoes, noes, potatoes, tomatoes, tornadoes, torpedoes, vetoes.

Exercise 1 •

Write sentences to illustrate the meaning of any six of the words above that are new to you.

> For example:
>
> Calicoes are not used much now in dressmaking because we have so many modern cheap fabrics.

1 _____

_____ (2)

2 _____

_____ (2)

3 _____

_____ (2)

4 _____

_____ (2)

5 _____

_____ (2)

6 _____

_____ (2)

Exercise 2

Write the correct plural form of the words in brackets.

1 The (**mosquito**) were very troublesome in Italy this year.

_____ (1)

2 Would you like some (**potato**) and (**tomato**)?

_____   _____ (2)

3 All three dance (**studio**) were in use so we had to rehearse in the school hall.

_____ (1)

4 On holiday this year we had fun wearing (**kimono**), (**poncho**) and (**sombrero**).

_____ _____ _____ (3)

5 The (**alto**) in the choir were accompanied by the (**cello**) in both (**oratorio**).

_____ _____ _____ (3)

6 The journalists struggled with the news (**embargo**) although the lava continued
to gush out of the three (**volcano**).

_____   _____ (2)

7 My grandfather kept his (**curio**) in the (**gazebo**) he had built in his garden.

_____   _____ (2)

8 We heard several (**cuckoo**) this morning but could get no (**photo**) of them.

_____   _____ (2)

Ignoble is an unusual word. It is formed by adding an
ig- prefix to noble. It means the opposite of noble.

Pronounce, pronounced, pronouncing, and so on, but
pronunciation (no o with the u).

The Latin words for one to ten

one: *unus* (or *una* or *unum*) two: *duo* (or *duae* or *duo*)

three: *tres* (or *tria*) four: *quattuor* five: *quinque* six: *sex*

seven: *septem* eight: *octem* nine: *novem* ten: *decem*

Note these are cardinal numbers. We will look at ordinal numbers (first, second, third, and so on) in a later exercise.

Knowing the origin of these words may help you to spell them correctly.

Exercise 1 •••••••••••••••••••••••

Write sentences to show the meaning of the following words, which have all come into English from the Latin words for the first ten ordinal numbers:

1 unite

_____

_____ (2)

2 triangular

_____

_____ (2)

3 decade

_____

_____ (2)

4 septet

_____

_____ (2)

5 octagon

_____

_____ (2)

6 quins

_____

_____ (2)

Exercise 2

These five words all come from *unus* (or *una* or *unum*), the Latin word for one. Make notes on what they mean and work out how they relate to 'oneness', using a good dictionary if you need to. Finally check that you can spell them all.

1 union

_____

_____

_____ (3)

2 unit

_____

_____

_____ (3)

3 unison

_____

_____

_____ (3)

4 unique

_____

_____

_____ (3)

5 unisex

_____

_____

_____ (3)

September, October, November and *December* were originally the seventh, eighth, ninth and tenth months, hence their names. Then Roman emperors Julius Caesar and Caesar Augustus put July and August, named after themselves, into the summer. That pushed the last four months of the year back to ninth, tenth, eleventh and twelfth positions.

Latin prepositions and adverbs

Many English words have their roots in Latin, the language used by the Romans.

A prefix is a letter or group of letters that forms the beginning of a word.

Knowing some Latin prefixes – which are often prepositions or adverbs – will help you to unravel the meaning and spelling of many English words.

Trans is the Latin word for across. Translate means to move meaning *across* to another language. A transatlantic airline carries passengers *across* the ocean to and from America.

Super is the Latin word for above or over. A supervisor has a position of responsibility *over* others. A supersized chocolate bar is *above* all the others because it is large.

Ante is the Latin word for before. An antenatal class helps parents *before* the birth of their baby. An anteroom is an area that you wait in *before* you go into a more important room.

Exercise •

1 Write the meaning of these words as briefly and clearly as you can.

transfusion: _____ (1)

transfer: _____ (1)

transit: _____ (1)

insuperable: _____ (1)

superfluous: _____ (1)

superimpose: _____ (1)

antepenultimate: _____ (1)

anterior: _____ (1)

2 Learn the spellings of these eight words. Then, working with a partner, take it in turns to test each other, or ask an adult to test you.

> The prefix ante- means before (anteroom, antenatal).
> Do not confuse it with anti- which means against
> (antibiotics, anti-foxhunting).

Words starting with gn-

Some (gnat, gnash, gnaw) of the small group of English words that begin with a silent **g-** date back to Old English, the language spoken in Britain before the Norman invasion of 1066 which, eventually, merged Old English with Latin-based French.

Others come from Greek. Gnosis, for example, means knowledge about spiritual truths.

The word gnocchi – potato dumplings – comes from Italian and gnu – another word for a wildebeest – comes from Xhosa, which is an African language.

Exercise ●

Using a dictionary to help you, fill in the gaps in the following sentences. Each answer is a word beginning with **gn-**.

1 We watched the shadow created by the _____ on the sundial as our watches crept towards midday. (1)

2 My granny collects colourful plastic _____ which sit in groups in her garden as if they were chatting. (1)

3 We took our bird books when we went to America and were delighted to spot lots of _____. (1)

4 Very elderly people sometimes have _____ hands, especially if they suffer from arthritis. (1)

5 The lowest point in your jaw is known to doctors and anatomists as the _____. (1)

6 _____ anxiety is common before exams and tests, especially if you should have revised but haven't! (1)

A *metre* is a unit of measurement (100 centimetres or 1000 millimetres) or another name for rhythm in, for example, poetry. (American English spells it meter.) In British English a *meter* is a measuring device such as a water meter.

Words ending in -mn

A handful of English words end with **mn** – but the **n** is silent. Autumn and column are examples.

However, when these words become another part of speech or take another form – autumnal or columnist, for instance – you can often hear the **n**, which might help you to remember that it's there.

Exercise 1 •

Write the words ending in -mn that match these definitions:

1 A song used in churches and school assemblies: _____ (1)

2 To express strong disapproval: _____ (1)

3 To send to hell or write something or someone off: _____ (1)

4 Very serious: _____ (1)

5 Paint or draw: _____ (1)

6 To regard scornfully: _____ (1)

Exercise 2 •

Now write your own definitions for these words:

1 solemnity

_____

_____ (2)

2 damnation

_____

_____ (2)

3 hymnal

_____

_____ (2)

4 condemnatory

_____

_____ (2)

Words ending in -cious

Many English adjectives end in **c-i-o-u-s**, which sounds like 'sherss' in speech: precious, gracious, vicious, for example. If you can learn the sequence of letters (remember: **Call In On Uncle Sam** – if it helps) it will ensure that you can spell quite a lot of tricky words correctly.

Exercise 1 •

Fill in the gaps in these sentences with words ending in **-cious**. The words you need are listed below.

suspicious   audacious   ferocious   atrocious   fallacious   capacious

1 That _____ dog has bitten so many postmen that now no one will deliver to the house. (1)

2 It is _____ to assume that everything you see in the night sky is a star. (1)

3 _____ weather for the whole of the Christmas holiday meant that we spent a lot of time indoors reading books. (1)

4 I knew the policeman was _____ because he questioned the girl who lives on the corner three times. (1)

5 The boot in our new car is much less _____ than the one in our old car, which was generally bigger. (1)

6 Professional divers have to be much more _____ than most of us are. (1)

Exercise 2 •

Find six more words ending in **-cious** and put them in sentences of your own to show that you understand their meaning.

1 _____ (2)

2 _____ (2)

3 _____ (2)

4 _____ (2)

5 _____ (2)

6 _____ (2)

Dis- or diss- ?

A number of words in English begin with **dis-**.

If the root word that **dis-** is attached to begins with **s** then we get a double **s**: dis+satisfy gives dissatisfy and dis+service gives disservice.

But if the root word does *not* begin with **s** then the **s** in **dis-** usually remains single: dis+appear gives disappear and dis+loyal gives disloyal.

Exercise ●

Write the **dis-** words formed from these roots:

1 count _____ (1)

2 cover _____ (1)

3 similar _____ (1)

4 appoint _____ (1)

5 infect _____ (1)

6 grace _____ (1)

7 solve _____ (1)

8 like _____ (1)

9 place _____ (1)

10 regard _____ (1)

11 simulate _____ (1)

12 use _____ (1)

> Don't forget to look up and learn the meanings of any of these words that are new to you.

> The verb/noun *travel* has a single l. But the l doubles (in British English) when the word takes other forms such as *travelled* or *traveller*.

> *Benefited* has only one t unlike *fitted*, which has two.

Dictation for spelling practice

Dictation can be a very useful way of memorising and practising spellings.

First you study the passage carefully, making sure that you can spell all the words. Then you get someone to read it aloud to you in short sections, usually repeating each section at least twice, while you write it down. Of course, you don't refer to the written passage while you are writing it down.

For many pupils, this is a more effective way of learning spellings than by using lists because the words are in a context, which is often helpful.

Exercise •

Try this dictation passage; using the instructions above.

Fourteen grateful but frightened picnickers were rescued today from a beautiful spot on one of the principal mountain passes in Austria. They had the dreadful experience of seeing a vehicle, completely out of control, careering towards them. The driver panicked but fortunately a skilful passenger grabbed the steering wheel and managed to brake just in time. Everyone concerned, including two unconscious men, was taken to a neighbouring hospital to be checked over.

_____

_____

_____

_____

_____

_____

_____

_____

_____

_____

_____

_____ (5)

Silent letters within eight tricky words

Many words in English include letters which are part of the spelling but which do not sound when they are spoken so they have to be learned and remembered. See, for example:

library	muscle	liaise	listen
orchestra	receipt	debt	obscene

Exercise ●

Write each of these eight words out carefully to make sure you can spell them with confidence. Now use the space below to devise a small crossword, wordsearch or other sort of puzzle to which these eight words are the answers. Then try it out on a friend or family member.

_____ (1) _____ (1) _____ (1)

_____ (1) _____ (1) _____ (1)

_____ (1) _____ (1)

One n or two?

We often use **un-** as a prefix to reverse the meaning of a word.

> For example: lined, unlined; memorable, unmemorable

If the word that is being changed begins with an **n** (necessary, unnecessary; natural, unnatural) then the original **n** remains and we spell the word with a double **n**.

If the base word starts with any letter other than **n** then the **un-** word has only a single **n**.

Exercise 1 ●

Write the **un-** form of these words.

1 missable	_____ (1)	2 noticed	_____ (1)
3 load	_____ (1)	4 listed	_____ (1)
5 observed	_____ (1)	6 numbered	_____ (1)
7 moved	_____ (1)	8 nerve	_____ (1)
9 known	_____ (1)	10 naturally	_____ (1)

Exercise 2 ●

Use each of the ten **un-** words you have formed in a sentence of your own.

1 _____ (2)

2 _____ (2)

3 _____ (2)

4 _____ (2)

5 _____ (2)

6 _____ (2)

7 _____ (2)

8 _____ (2)

9 _____ (2)

10 _____ (2)

-full, -fully and -ful

Many adjectives and nouns in English are formed by adding the suffix **-ful** to a noun.

> To be wonderful means to be full of wonder and to be fearful means to be full of fear.

Note that although we use full and fully as separate words, the adjectival suffix **-ful** has only one **l**.

> Hence houseful and fearful.

Also note that nouns ending in **-y** change the **-y** to an **i** before taking the **-ful** suffix.

> Hence beauty becomes beautiful and pity becomes pitiful.

Adverbs in English are usually formed by adding **-ly** to an adjective. That means that if you form an adverb from a **-ful** adjective you get two **l**'s. For example:

Noun	Adjective	Adverb
doubt	doubtful	doubtfully
force	forceful	forcefully

Get into the habit of spelling by building a word up from its base:

appear, appear/ance, dis/appear/ance

care, care/less, care/less/ly

hurry, hurr/ied, hurr/ied/ly, un/hurr/ied/ly

and so on.

Exercise

List ten nouns that take **-ful** when they become adjectives. Then write the adjectival and adverbial forms, taking care to spell them correctly.

Noun	Adjective	Adverb	
			(3)
			(3)
			(3)
			(3)
			(3)
			(3)
			(3)
			(3)
			(3)
			(3)

Skill and *skilled* each have a double l but *skilful* (in British English) has only one in the middle. *Will* and *wilful* work in the same way.

Enrol has only one l in British English (Americans spell it with two). *Enrolling* and *enrolled* have a double l in all forms of English.

Spill and *spell* each have a double l. The past tense can be *spilt* or *spelt*, both of which have a single l. But if you used the alternative past tense, *spilled* or *spelled*, then the l remains doubled.

Ordinal numbers

English	Latin	English	Latin
first	*primus*	second	*secundus*
third	*tertius*	fourth	*quartus*
fifth	*quintus*	sixth	*sextus*
seventh	*septimus*	eighth	*octavus*
ninth	*nonus*	tenth	*decimus*

Exercise ●

Study the table carefully. Now work out the answers to the following questions.

1 What do we call the three stages of education in Britain and why?

_____

_____

_____ (2)

2 When statisticians use quartiles, how many groups are they working with?

_____ (2)

3 When families were larger, Tertius and Septimus were quite common names. Which children do you think got them?

_____ (2)

4 How many decimetres are there in a metre?

_____ (2)

5 Nonanoic acid, a sort of paraffin, is used in medicines, lacquers and plastics. What do you think is paraffin's position in the methane table used by professional chemists?

_____ (2)

6 If you are told to quintuplicate something, what will you do to it?

_____ (2)

7 How often does a sexennial event occur?

_____ (2)

8 Octavo is a printing term referring to book size. How many times is the paper folded to produce an octavo book format?

_____ (2)

More Latin prepositions

> **inter-** means between (international, interschool).
>
> **intra-** means within (intranet).
>
> **sub-** means under (subway, submarine).

Remembering these will help you to sort out the meaning and spelling of a large number of words, as well as showing you how words have evolved and how they relate to each other.

Exercise 1 •

Fill in the gaps in these sentences with words that use the prepositions listed above.

1 A school's website, usually accessible only to pupils, staff and perhaps parents is known as

its _____. (1)

2 When our extension was built, the builder _____ part of the work to

specialists. (1)

3 Because our class is so large, we are often _____ into smaller groups. (1)

4 _____ activities are those that take place inside, or within, the walls of a

school or college. (1)

5 I _____ Mrs Ewart on her way to break because I wanted to catch her

before she spoke to other staff. (1)

6 We were told to use _____ in our notes about volcanoes because the

teacher wanted us to focus separately on each aspect of the topic. (1)

Exercise 2 •

Use a dictionary to help you find four more words that relate to the Latin prepositions **inter**, **intra** or **sub** and use them in sentences of your own.

1 _____

_____ (2)

2 _____

_____ (2)

3 _____

_____ (2)

4 _____

_____ (2)

Homographs

Homographs are words that are spelled the same but have different meanings and are usually pronounced differently. Effectively they are language coincidences and rather fun.

> Consider for example the **lead** pipe used as a murder weapon in the game Cluedo alongside your decision to **lead** the way when you went on a country walk. Then there's the **content** of your history essay compared with how **content** you feel when you get a good mark for it. **Polish** with an upper-case initial letter describes a person or item from Poland, but with a lower-case initial letter **polish** is what you put on wooden furniture to make it shine.

Exercise

Which homographs are the answers to these double clues?

1 abandon/a remote dry place where few plants can grow: _____ (1)

2 sick person/describes a pass or ticket that doesn't work for some reason such as being out of date: _____ (1)

3 item/verb meaning to express disapproval: _____ (1)

4 to write your name again/to give up a job or position: _____ (1)

5 rubbish/verb expressing a decision not to do something: _____ (1)

6 history, geography or maths, for example/verb meaning to impose something on someone: _____ (1)

> Neighbour's *refuse* to be put in the bin. Neighbours *refuse* to be put in the bin. Yes, homographs are fun and an apostrophe can make a lot of difference.

> *Affect* is a verb meaning to have an influence on. Remember: animals *affect* agriculture. *Effect* is (almost always) a noun meaning influence so it generally has 'the' in front of it. Remember: The *effect* was extraordinary.

Words ending in -tious

Quite a large group of English adjectives end in **-tious**. You have to separate these in your mind from the words that end in **-cious** because the 'sherss' sound is the same.

Exercise ●

Make up crossword-style clues to which these eight **-tious** words are the answers. Be as cryptic and clever as you wish. You can create the crossword in the box below.

1 ambitious: _____ (2)

2 cautious: _____ (2)

3 conscientious: _____ (2)

4 nutritious: _____ (2)

5 superstitious: _____ (2)

6 pretentious: _____ (2)

7 infectious: _____ (2)

8 fictitious: _____ (2)

-able or -ible?

Some adjectives end in **-able** (irritable, workable, doable) and others in **-ible** (responsible, divisible, edible). There is, unfortunately, no easy rule about this to help you and, in general, these are spellings that you simply have to learn – although the **-able** ending is more common than the **-ible** one. If you have to guess you are much more likely to be right with **-able** than with **-ible**.

Exercise •

Fill in the gaps in these sentences, using a dictionary to help you when you need to. After you've done the exercise it would also be worth spending ten minutes committing these spellings to memory.

1 The speaker's voice was almost inaud_____. (1)

2 Meat and fish are perish_____ foods. (1)

3 Ella and Ruby are insepar_____ friends. (1)

4 Are you respons_____ for this mess? (1)

5 Twenty is divis_____ by five. (1)

6 When is that bill pay_____. (1)

7 Most people record memo_____ events by photographing them. (1)

8 The summer heat in southern Spain is bear_____ as long as you don't hurry. (1)

9 Since I took to typing most of my work my handwriting has become much less leg_____. (1)

10 My sister is very flex_____ because she's been dancing since she was a toddler. (1)

11 'Your performance in rugby is laugh_____,' said the PE teacher, crossly. (1)

12 The idea of work experience is to make young people more employ_____. (1)

> When you add -able to a word ending in -e to form an adjective the -e usually disappears. Hence *forgive/* becomes *forgivable, dispose/ disposable* and, *argue/ arguable*.

Six tricky words

Look carefully at these words and learn their spellings:

- occurrence (double **c** and double **r**)
- receive (ei in the middle)
- grateful (**-ate-** in the middle and single **l** at the end)
- preferred (double **r**)
- immediately (double **m** and **-ate-** before **-ly**)
- noisily (vowels are **-o- -i- -i-**; the y from 'noisy' has gone)

Exercise •

Make up a paragraph that uses all six of these words. Then, working with a partner, take turns to dictate your paragraphs to each other so that you both practise writing the words correctly spelt.

_____

_____

_____

_____

_____

_____

_____

_____

_____

_____

_____

_____ (6)

Awkward is the only work in English that includes a k sandwiched by two w's.

Diarrhoea is a nasty thing to have. It's also tricky to spell. Here's a neat way of remembering it: _Dash in a rush, run hard or expect accident._

Synonyms

English is a very rich language. It has far more words than, for example, French, German or Italian. That is why we often have a number of words that mean the same thing, or nearly the same thing. Words with similar meanings are called synonyms.

For example:

> Pursue, follow, chase, stalk, track and shadow (as verbs) all mean to go or run after someone or something.
>
> Silent, still, hushed, inaudible, noiseless, soundless, peaceful and tranquil are all adjectives meaning quiet.

Take care though. It is rare for two words to mean exactly the same. Think of synonyms as words that are similar in meaning rather than being identical.

Exercise •

Supply another word close in meaning for the words in bold in these sentences. Try to do this without looking anything up, but if you get stuck a thesaurus will help you.

1 We would like to express our **sincere** gratitude for what you did. _____ (1)

2 That goal was **superb**. _____ (1)

3 Granny makes **nice** cakes. _____ (1)

4 Have you **finished** your homework? _____ (1)

5 Our swimming **teacher** is very good. _____ (1)

6 The trio stood in triumph at the **summit** of Mont Blanc. _____ (1)

7 The thief **stole** three computers from our house. _____ (1)

8 I want this room **tidy** when I come back. _____ (1)

All right is always two separate words.

Ph words

Ph – pronounced like **f** – occurs in English spelling in some words. Most have developed from Ancient Greek. It can come at the beginning (phrase), in the middle (alphabet) or at the end (telegraph). Some words even have it twice (photograph).

The word graph – a written chart – comes from the Greek word for writing and many English words include the letters **g-r-a-p-h**. All are loosely connected to writing although many have moved some distance from their original meaning. Geography, for instance, is literally writing about the earth. An autograph is something you write yourself and a biography is writing about a person's life. And graphite is a mined form of carbon with which you can make marks so it is used in pencils – for writing.

Some first names, originally Greek, include **ph** too: Phoebe and Persephone, for example.

Exercise ●

Solve these clues. Each answer is a word including **ph**. The words you need are given below. Research your answers using an encyclopaedia or the internet if you need to.

apostrophe	amphibian	pharmacy	Stephen	pharaoh
epitaph	symphony	elephant	choreography	phobia

1 A deep fear of something: _____ (1)

2 A shop, or part of one, where you can collect prescription drugs: _____ (1)

3 First Christian martyr whose saint's day is 26 December: _____ (1)

4 Punctuation mark that shows possession or omission: _____ (1)

5 The world's largest pachyderm: _____ (1)

6 Arrangement of dance moves in a stage show: _____ (1)

7 Animal that can breathe both in air and water: _____ (1)

8 A king in Ancient Egypt: _____ (1)

9 Long piece of music, usually in four sections, played by an orchestra: _____ (1)

10 Statement about a dead person, summing up his or her life, often on a gravestone:

_____ (1)

Practise or practice?

Read these two sentences aloud:

> I advise you to apologise.
>
> My advice is that you should apologise.

In the first, advise is a verb. In the second, advice is a noun and you are very unlikely to confuse them because they are pronounced differently.

The words practise/practice follow exactly the same rule, although they sound the same. Practise is a verb and practice is a noun.

> I should practise the piano more than I do.
>
> Cricket practice is held on Tuesdays.

Note that American English does not follow this rule.

Another word that does something similar in British English is license/licence.

> I must renew my television licence.
>
> You may only own a gun if you license it.

Look carefully at related words such as practises, practising, practices, licensing, licensed and licenses.

Exercise ●●●●●●●●●●●●●●●●●●●●●●●●●●●●

Fill in the gaps in these sentences using the words discussed above.

1 My grandparents have held their driving _____ since the 1960s. (1)

2 Your playing is so much better that I can tell you've been _____. (1)

3 This restaurant is not _____ to sell alcohol. (1)

4 Let's have a _____ and see if we can improve our table tennis. (1)

5 Dr Sharp's medical _____ covers three villages. (1)

6 My uncle has been a _____ solicitor for twenty years. (1)

7 You no longer have to buy a _____ for a dog in Britain. (1)

8 The Driver and Vehicle _____ Agency for Britain is based in Swansea. (1)

Poly- and tele-

Learning the meaning of two prefixes that have come from Greek will help you to make sense of a number of English words.

> **Poly** means much or many. (A polygon is a many-sided shape and a polyglot is someone who speaks many languages.)
>
> **Tele** means distant (telephone, telescope).

Note that neither prefix includes any double letters.

Exercise 1 •

Choose the correct words from the list below to fill the gaps in these sentences.

polygamy   polyphonic   polytechnic   polymath   telegraph   telepathy   television

1 There is a sort of _____ between my parents, who always seem to know what the other is thinking. (1)

2 Cultures that practise _____ often say that it is a good way of allowing a man to take care of more than one woman. (1)

3 _____ music has many different tunes played at the same time and woven together. (1)

4 Our teacher, Miss Clift, is quite a _____ because she speaks Italian, Greek and Russian as well as playing piano and double bass and teaching us maths. (1)

5 When John Logie Baird made the first _____ connection it seemed almost unbelievable that cameras could allow people to see far-off events. (1)

6 My uncle studied at Woolwich _____, which offered a wide range of subjects, before it became part of a university. (1)

7 The wires that link landline phones are still carried round Britain on _____ poles. (1)

Exercise 2 •

Now write your own definitions for these words:

_____

_____

_____ (5)

kn and gh

English has a handful of words that begin with **kn** (knife, knee) and with **gh** (ghost, ghastly). Most of these come from Old English, the language spoken here before the arrival of the Normans with French in 1066 and which gradually merged with Old English.

Some words – also mostly from Old English – have **gh** elsewhere in the word (laugh, night), where it is usually either silent or sounds like **f**.

Exercise •

Use these ten words in sentences of your own to show you understand their meaning. Take care to spell them correctly.

1 knack

_____

_____

_____ (2)

2 knead

_____

_____

_____ (2)

3 knuckle

_____

_____

_____ (2)

4 knowledgeable

_____

_____

_____ (2)

5 gherkin

_____

_____

_____ (2)

6 ghetto

_____

_____

_____ (2)

7 freight

_____

_____

_____ (2)

8 distraught

_____

_____

_____ (2)

9 drought

_____

_____

_____ (2)

10 wheelwright

_____

_____

_____ (2)

Three gh- words that *don't* come from Old English:

- *ghee* is clarified butter used in Indian cooking and comes from Hindi
- a *ghazi* is a Muslim fighter and comes from Arabic
- *Ghent* is a city in Flemish-speaking Belgium.

-ys or -ies

There are very few reliable spelling rules in English, but here's one that almost always works.

If a noun or a verb ends in **-y** and has a vowel before it then you simply add **s** when you make it plural or change the verb form. For example:

Nouns	
monkey	monkeys
Monday	Mondays
boy	boys
Verbs	
Market traders display their goods.	Every market trader displays his or her goods.
Schools employ teachers.	Our school employs teachers.

But if the **-y** which ends the noun or verb is preceded by a consonart then the **y** goes and we use **-ies** instead. For example:

Nouns	
nursery	nurseries
lady	ladies
Verbs	
We have to query those figures.	We'll wait while he queries those figures.
I pity him.	He pities me.

Exercise 1 ●

Add the correct form of the word in brackets to these sentences.

1 When I take music exams Mrs Ericson _____ me. (**accompany**) (1)

2 Judas _____ Jesus in many paintings. (**betray**) (1)

3 When my father _____ information he does it very clearly. (**convey**) (1)

4 We made our _____ in writing. (**apology**) (1)

Answers

-os or oes? (page 6)

Exercise 1
For example:

Buffaloes live naturally in huge herds on plains.

I often play dominoes with my grandpa because it's a game that can be enjoyed at any age.

Politicians sometimes apply trade embargoes to countries they don't want anyone to do business with.

There were a number of full-voiced jingoes at the anti-immigration meeting.

Sixteenth-century European explorers first discovered both potatoes and tomatoes in South America.

Vetoes from teachers sometimes limit the power of school councils.

Exercise 2
1 mosquitoes
2 potatoes, tomatoes
3 studios
4 kimonos, ponchos, sombreros
5 altos, cellos, oratorios
6 embargoes, volcanoes
7 curios, gazebos
8 cuckoos, photos

The Latin words for one to ten (page 8)

Exercise 1
For example:

1 In the last 50 years the European Union has gradually built up as more countries have seen why it makes sense to unite.
2 The shopping centre at Bluewater in Kent is triangular with a major store at each of the three corners.
3 As the first decade of the century ended in 2010 people were already getting excited about the 2012 London Olympics and Paralympics.
4 Jazz is sometimes played by seven players who form a septet.
5 Part of the opera house at Buxton in Derbyshire is known as The Octagon for its eight sides.
6 Five live babies born at once is very rare but there have been several famous sets of quins who have all survived.

Exercise 2
1 A group that acts for the benefit of its members, such as a trade union. The group acts as *one* organisation as if were an individual.
2 A single entity – could be a set of work within the school curriculum or a measurement such as a unit of electricity. It always means *one* single item, often as part of something larger.
3 The term given to singers all singing the same notes rather than harmonising. We sing the hymn 'in unison'. The choir sings as if it were *one* person.
4 Only *one* of something in existence. So Ayers Rock and the Grand Canyon are unique. Note that because unique means only *one* it is never correct to say 'rather unique' or 'very unique'. Something is either unique or it isn't.
5 Applies to both sexes – treats them as *one* whole group without separation. Hence, unisex hairdressers or toilets are for use by both females and males.

Latin prepositions and adverbs (page 10)

Exercise
transfusion: the movement of donor blood into a patient

transfer: to move something/someone from one place to another

transit: the state of being moved

insuperable: describes something (e.g. a difficulty) which cannot be overcome

superfluous: unnecessary because there is already plenty of whatever it is

superimpose: to force something (e.g. a set of rules or a drawing) over something which is already there

antepenultimate: third from last (e.g. October is the antepenultimate month)

anterior: at the front of something

Words starting with gn- (page 11)

Exercise
1 gnomon
2 gnomes
3 gnatcatchers
4 gnarled
5 gnathion
6 Gnawing

Words ending in -mn (page 12)

Exercise 1
1 hymn
2 condemn
3 damn
4 solemn
5 limn
6 contemn

Exercise 2
For example:
1 seriousness or gravity
2 sending of a person to hell or some other undesirable place
3 collection or book of hymns
4 describes something disapproving

Words ending in -cious (page 13)

Exercise 1
1 ferocious
2 fallacious
3 Atrocious
4 suspicious
5 capacious
6 audacious

Exercise 2
Possibilities include: conscious, unconscious, malicious, luscious, judicious, pernicious, avaricious, spacious, vivacious, voracious, tenacious, pugnacious, officious.

Dis- or diss- ? (page 14)

Exercise
1 discount
2 discover
3 dissimilar
4 disappoint
5 disinfect
6 disgrace
7 dissolve
8 dislike
9 displace
10 disregard
11 dissimulate
12 disuse

Dictation for spelling practice (page 15)

Exercise
No answers applicable

Silent letters within eight tricky words (page 16)

Exercise
No answers applicable

One n or two? (page 17)

Exercise 1
1 unmissable
2 unnoticed
3 unload
4 unlisted
5 unobserved
6 unnumbered
7 unmoved
8 unnerve
9 unknown
10 unnaturally

Exercise 2
For example:
1 In her scarlet wig my sister was unmissable even in a crowd.
2 I tried, but failed, to slip unnoticed into the back row when I hoped Mrs Tyson was not looking.
3 It is a tedious job to unload the groceries from the car after a supermarket trip.
4 The library book I wanted was unlisted so I couldn't borrow it.
5 The burglar slipped unobserved into the building.
6 The houses in our road are unnumbered, which sometimes confuses visitors.
7 Most people in the class shed a tear but I was unmoved by the play.
8 The key to winning at rugby is to unnerve your opponents.
9 The tomb of the unknown warrior is in Westminster Abbey.
10 Rather unnaturally, many foxes now live in cities and feed on human detritus.

-full, -fully and -ful (page 18)

Exercise
For example:

Noun	Adjective	Adverb
art	artful	artfully
cheer	cheerful	cheerfully
deceit	deceitful	deceitfully
disgrace	disgraceful	disgracefully
duty	dutiful	dutifully
glee	gleeful	gleefully
hate	hateful	hatefully
hope	hopeful	hopefully
mercy	merciful	mercifully
peace	peaceful	peacefully
purpose	purposeful	purposefully
respect	respectful	respectfully
spite	spiteful	spitefully
thought	thoughtful	thoughtfully
tune	tuneful	tunefully
waste	wasteful	wastefully
youth	youthful	youthfully

Ordinal numbers (page 20)

<u>Exercise</u>
1 Primary, secondary and tertiary. It means first, second and third stages from the Latin words *primus*, *secundus* and *tertius*.
2 Four
3 Tertius was usually the third child or son and Septimus the seventh.
4 Ten
5 Ninth
6 Multiply it by five
7 Every six years
8 Eight

More Latin prepositions (page 21)

<u>Exercise1</u>
1 intranet
2 subcontracted
3 subdivided
4 Intramural
5 intercepted
6 subheadings

<u>Exercise 2</u>
Possibilities include: interpose, intersect, interpret, intercede, intrastate, subcutaneous, subordinate, subdominant, submerge, subjugate.

Homographs (page 22)

<u>Exercise</u>
1 desert
2 invalid
3 object
4 resign
5 refuse
6 subject

Words ending in -tious (page 23)

<u>Exercise</u>
For example:
1 If this is how you are, then the sky's the limit.
2 Careful! Feline broken and sounds like you, stands before debts.
3 Diligent
4 Good for you
5 This is what you are if you won't walk under a ladder.
6 Opposite of modest
7 Catching
8 Made up

-able or -ible? (page 24)

<u>Exercise</u>
1 inaudible
2 perishable
3 inseparable
4 responsible
5 divisible
6 payable
7 memorable
8 bearable
9 legible
10 flexible
11 laughable
12 employable

Six tricky words (page 25)

<u>Exercise</u>
For example:

It was a rare occurrence for us to receive even a letter from Aunt Jane in New Zealand, so we were grateful when she sent us a box of presents. Although we would have preferred items better suited to our ages, we immediately wrote to thank her – despite my young brother crying noisily because there wasn't anything suitable for him.

Synonyms (page 26)

<u>Exercise</u>
For example:

1 wholehearted, heartfelt, deep, real
2 excellent, outstanding, first-rate, perfect
3 lovely, delicious, fine, wonderful, tasty
4 completed, finalised, done
5 instructor, trainer, coach
6 top, peak, apex, tip
7 took, purloined, nicked, filched
8 neat, organised, orderly, immaculate

Ph words (page 27)

<u>Exercise</u>
1 phobia
2 pharmacy
3 Stephen
4 apostrophe
5 elephant
6 choreography
7 amphibian
8 pharaoh
9 symphony
10 epitaph

Practise or practice? (page 28)

Exercise
1 licences
2 practising
3 licensed
4 practice
5 practice
6 practising
7 licence
8 Licensing

Poly- and tele- (page 29)

Exercise 1
1 telepathy
2 polygamy
3 Polyphonic
4 polymath
5 television
6 Polytechnic
7 telegraph

Exercise 2
For example:

thermometer, thermostat, thermal, thermodynamic, thermos (flask), therm (unit of gas)

kn and gh (page 30)

Exercise
For example:

1 My mother has a knack with hats, which is why she looks so good in them.
2 The more energetically you knead the dough with your fists the better the bread will be.
3 It is time to knuckle down to some hard work.
4 Great Uncle Bob is extraordinarily knowledgeable about whales and other marine mammals.
5 There is a building in London shaped like a pickled cucumber, which is why it is nicknamed 'The Gherkin'.
6 In Warsaw during the Second World War, Jews were not allowed to move freely round the city and were forced to live in a ghetto.
7 Most freight arrives in Britain by sea and then travels by road to distribution depots.
8 When our beloved dog disappeared we were all distraught.
9 Alternating drought and heavy rain makes life very difficult for farmers.
10 There is a traditional wheelwright in our village, making old-fashioned cart wheels.

-ys or -ies (page 32)

Exercise 1
1 accompanies
2 betrays
3 conveys
4 apologies
5 theories
6 supplies
7 Butterflies
8 Lorries
9 quays
10 applies

Exercise 2
1 (a) donkeys
  (b) jellies
  (c) stories
  (d) storeys
  (e) puppies
  (f) armies
  (g) trolleys
  (h) trays
  (i) luxuries
  (j) delays
  (k) alloys
  (l) valleys
2 (a) party
  (b) study
  (c) convoy
  (d) spray
  (e) berry
  (f) wiseguy

The silent p (page 34)

Exercise 1
1 pseudonym
2 psalm
3 psoriasis
4 ptarmigan
5 pneumatic
6 psychiatrist

Exercise 2
For example:

1 Some authors use a pseudonym to conceal their identity.
2 Psalm 23, which begins 'The Lord is my shepherd', is probably the most famous.
3 Psoriasis is a distressing skin condition, which causes flakiness and itching.
4 We enjoyed watched the ptarmigans during our Arctic cruise.
5 Modern pneumatic tyres on cars need to be replaced about every 30 000 miles.
6 My sister suffers from serious depression but Mr Agate, her psychiatrist, has helped her a lot.

Words ending in -re (page 35)

Exercise 1
Possibilities include:

euchre (a traditional board game)

fibre (tough bits in vegetables, grain, and so on)

metre (unit of measurement)

ochre (yellow)

ogre (giant)

philtre (love potion)

sabre (short bladed weapon)

sombre (dark and serious)

Another dictation
No answers applicable

-fy words (page 36)

Exercise 1
1 notify
2 glorify
3 terrify
4 intensify
5 classify
6 certify
7 crucify
8 pacify
9 electrify
10 horrify

Exercise 2
1 To become rotten (usually flesh).
2 To make holy – churches, for instance, have to be sanctified by special prayers.
3 To give evidence in court.
4 To make solid – ice is solidified water.
5 Literally to turn to stone; now usually means to frighten.
6 To make stupid; now usually means to make someone stop functioning mentally, for example by drugging or hitting them.

Words with -cei- (page 37)

Exercise 1
1 receipt
2 deceitful
3 inconceivable
4 perceived, misconceived
5 undeceived
6 ceilinged

Exercise 2
These are a starting point; there may be more:

meant, hive, achieve, time, chive, itch, mine, chime, etch, vine, chit, vain, vetch, vent, heave, vein, vehement, cave, mean, tame, mace, neat, mate, cant, team, have, thieve, thin, mint, hint, event, match, cinema, teach, each, teen, ache, even, haven, heaven, mane, main, thee, then, than, them, thane, heat, methane, niche

Word wheels (page 38)

Exercise 1
For example: surprised, uprise, upside, prise, press, super, spire, spied, purse, pride, prude, pied, pies, pure, errs, used, ripe, ruse, ride, rude, side, sire, dupe, dress, dies

Exercise 2
No answers applicable

-ist words (page 39)

Exercise 1
1 flautist
2 atheist
3 dramatist
4 humorist
5 plagiarist
6 ventriloquist
7 geologist
8 novelist
9 idealist
10 numismatist

Exercise 2
No answers applicable

The silent b (page 40)

Exercise 1
For example: bomb, catacomb, climb, crumb, debt, debtor, doubt, doubter, doubtful, limb, numb, plumb, plumber, subtle, subtly, thumb, womb

Exercise 2
No answers applicable

When -ei- says 'ay' (page 41)

Exercise
For example:

Eight neighbouring, reigning sheiks took the weight of their freight on a sleigh. So much did it weigh that the veins stood out on their veiled faces as they pulled the reins.

Mal- and ben- (page 42)

<u>Exercise</u>
For example:

1 When well-used trainers become malodorous you can get rid of the smell by putting them in the washing machine.
2 We were afraid that the growth on Dad's face was cancer and very relieved when it turned out to be benign.
3 Our school has had many benefactors over the years, one of whom gave us enough money to rebuild the science rooms.
4 I thought I had athlete's foot on my toes but the doctor told me it was a completely different malady.
5 Malnutrition is a huge problem in much of Africa where people are simply too poor to feed themselves healthily.
6 It was very unfair of the journalist to malign the lawyer who was only trying to do her job.
7 It is beneficial to health to eat five portions of fruit and vegetables each day.
8 In monasteries and convents monks and nuns used to bless visitors with prayers by reciting benisons.
9 My mother had a feeling of malaise when my elder brother kept staying out late at night without telling her why.
10 Armed robbers, murderers, arsonists and other malefactors are usually sent to prison.

-er or -or? (page 44)

<u>Exercise 1</u>
1 deserter
2 competitor
3 juror
4 astronomer
5 surveyor
6 ancestor
7 conductor
8 impersonator
9 smuggler
10 auditor

<u>Exercise 2</u>
1 vendor
2 perjurer
3 footballer
4 councillor
5 milliner
6 decorator
7 investor
8 chorister
9 pensioner
10 ambassador

Phobias (page 45)

<u>Exercise 1</u>
1 foreigners
2 heights
3 spiders
4 anything new
5 open spaces
6 crowds
7 darkness
8 flying

<u>Another word wheel activity</u>
For example: amble, lance, blame, beam, meal, male, able, cable, mule, blue, clue, ambulance

Antonyms (page 46)

<u>Exercise</u>
For example:

1 cowardly, feeble, spineless, lily-livered
2 contrast, foil, antithesis, clash
3 split, separate, diverge, disunite, divide
4 loud, noisy, deafening, resounding
5 impatience, irritation, restiveness, exasperation
6 unworried, confident, carefree, unconcerned

Double consonants in verbs (page 47)

<u>Exercise 1</u>
1 grinning, grinned
2 equalling, equalled
3 admitting, admitted
4 fulfilling, fulfilled
5 whipping, whipped
6 controlling, controlled
7 marring, marred
8 quitting, quitted
9 compelling, compelled
10 clapping, clapped

<u>Exercise 2</u>
No answers applicable

Easily confused endings (page 48)

<u>Exercise</u>
For example:

-ary	-ory	-ery	-ury
burglary	accessory	archery	century
commentary	category	bribery	injury
contrary	directory	cemetery	luxury
dictionary	dormitory	cookery	mercury
estuary	inventory	effrontery	penury
granary	laboratory	jewellery	
library	lavatory	machinery	
military	memory	recovery	
necessary	territory	slavery	
temporary	victory	snobbery	

Latin roots (page 49)

<u>Exercise 1</u>
For example:

1 Mark was put on report by his form tutor because he was guilty of rudeness, failure to work hard and various other transgressions.
2 Modern football fans sometimes get aggressive if their team has lost.
3 The Trades Union Congress, or TUC, is the central body that unites various trade unions.
4 My guitar playing has regressed since July because I haven't practised enough during the holidays.
5 I enjoyed Mrs Elton's long digression during English this morning because I had always wondered about Michael Morpurgo's own life.
6 Our dog's cancer got progressively worse and in the end the kindest thing was to have him put to sleep.

<u>Exercise 2</u>
For example: dormant, dormitory, dormouse

Prefixes that change their spellings (page 50)

<u>Exercise</u>
1 irreplaceable
2 illiterate
3 immortal
4 irrelevant
5 immobile
6 illegal
7 impious
8 irresponsible
9 illegible
10 impolite

More word wheels (page 51)

<u>Exercise 1</u>
For example: star, cater, later, rate, real, tear, stare, tare, rest, resat, earl, trace, escalator

<u>Exercise 2</u>
No answers applicable

Words with -fer- (page 52)

<u>Exercise 1</u>

Root word	-ed	-ing	-ence
refer	referred	referring	reference
infer	inferred	inferring	inference
confer	conferred	conferring	conference
defer	deferred	deferring	deference
prefer	preferred	preferring	preference

<u>Exercise 2</u>
For example: The conference deferred the decision about the transfer because the speaker, who preferred the option referred to by the chairman, made reference to the other man's inference.

Words that sometimes cause problems (page 53)

<u>Exercise</u>
For example:

My cousin George tends to be a bit conceited and there is usually an argument when his family visits ours. On more than one occasion his father or mine has come upstairs to separate George and me, telling us that there is no benefit in our trying to play together if all we do is quarrel. They are both very definite about this. Yet surely being able to rub along with your cousin is one of the necessities of life?

-duce, -pose, -struct and -clude (page 54)

<u>Exercise</u>
For example:

1 A conclusion, an idea formed after studying something – literally led from something else.
2 To speak badly of someone – literally to lead (for example) a reputation across to somewhere else.
3 To come between two people in a discussion – literally to place (something) between them.
4 To topple, for example a president – literally to put someone elsewhere.
5 Showing, as in the exposure of someone's lies – literally to put outside.
6 The placing of something or someone where it or he/she may not be required, for example the imposition of a rule or supervisor.
7 A misunderstanding – literally wrongly arranged.
8 A teacher or tutor – literally someone who arranges learning in someone else.
9 Closed off or quiet, for example a secluded spot.
10 To prevent or exclude – literally closed before, for example: We explored all rooms in the National Trust house except the ones from which we were precluded.

Homophones (page 56)

Exercise
For example:

1 'Which aisle are the eggs in?' I asked the supermarket manager.
  The Isle of Wight is the largest island off the south coast of England.
2 Waist bands get tight if you overeat.
  All rubbish should go in the waste paper bin.
3 A traditional wedding ring is a plain gold band.
  If you wash your clothes by hand you have to wring the water out of them.
4 My father doesn't often gamble but he usually has a bet on the World Cup.
  It is lovely to see a lively lamb gambol in a field.
5 I prefer coarse porridge to the smoother sort.
  A GCSE course usually ends in a formal exam.
6 If you buy something for a pound and sell it for more you have made a profit.
  Mohammed was Islam's great prophet.
7 It is illegal to steal other people's belongings.
  Stainless steel is a common material for kitchen equipment such as saucepans.
8 It is not sensible to hoard too much food because it might go off.
  The story of Ali Baba features a horde of brigands.
9 The first thing a bulb does when it starts to grow is to put down a root.
  The route from our house to yours includes five sets of traffic lights.
10 A traditional milkmaid carries two buckets on a yoke across her shoulders.
  The yolk of an egg is more nutritious than the white.

Some quirky plurals (page 58)

Exercise
1 radii
2 larvae
3 cacti
4 crises
5 criteria
6 oases
7 fungi
8 memoranda
9 phenomena
10 diagnoses

Eponyms (page 59)

Exercise
1 Francis Beaufort – the Beaufort scale
2 Amelia Bloomer – bloomers
3 Louis Braille – braille
4 John Langdon Down – Down's syndrome
5 Jean Nicot – nicotine
6 John Montagu, 4th Earl of Sandwich – sandwich

Short words for long (page 60)

Exercise
1 start
2 brave
3 try
4 drink
5 top
6 see
7 get/buy
8 sad
9 oil
10 ghosts

Does the e stay or go? (page 61)

Exercise 1
1 sincerely
2 pining
3 admiration
4 Fortunately
5 wisely
6 useful
7 separately
8 living
9 aching
10 nervous

Exercise 2
For example: Truly and duly the ninth argument is wholly awful.

Extending your vocabulary (page 62)

Exercise
For example:

1 J.K. Rowling's first crime novel after the Harry Potter books was written pseudonymously.
2 Although some people take it very seriously, astrology is generally regarded as a pseudoscience.
3 *David Copperfield* is a prime example of a nineteenth-century novel – an archetype.
4 A monarch is a single person at the head of a kingdom.
5 Photosynthesis is how plants use the energy in sunlight in order to thrive.
6 It must be terrible to suffer from photophobia and want to be in the dark all the time.
7 Religions such as Christianity, Islam and Judaism believe in one omnipotent god whose power is everything.
8 Goats, which will even eat paper bags given the chance, are famously omnivorous.
9 It is very helpful for a driver who cannot, for whatever reason, manage a clutch to use an automatic car, which changes gear by itself.
10 I don't have the autonomy to make that decision, which will have to be referred to the committee.

Words to watch (page 64)

Exercise
No answers applicable

5 How many different _____ are there about the causes of obesity? **(theory)** (1)

6 My father's business _____ raw materials for the motor industry. **(supply)** (1)

7 _____ live for only a few hours. **(butterfly)** (1)

8 _____ and cars stream past our house at all times of day and night. **(lorry)** (1)

9 The fish was sold fresh along both _____. **(quay)** (1)

10 Kieran Jones _____ for a new job at least once a year. **(apply)** (1)

Exercise 2

1 Write the plural form of these nouns:

(a) donkey _____ (1)

(b) jelly _____ (1)

(c) story _____ (1)

(d) storey _____ (1)

(e) puppy _____ (1)

(f) army _____ (1)

(g) trolley _____ (1)

(h) tray _____ (1)

(i) luxury _____ (1)

(j) delay _____ (1)

(k) alloy _____ (1)

(l) valley _____ (1)

2 Write the singular form of these nouns:

(a) parties _____ (1)

(b) studies _____ (1)

(c) convoys _____ (1)

(d) sprays _____ (1)

(e) berries _____ (1)

(f) wiseguys _____ (1)

Monies is a banking term. It is the plural of money and really, rather oddly, means sums of money. It is a very unusual exception to the y/ies rule.

The silent p

Some words start **ps-** (psychology), **pt-** (pterodactyl) or **pn-** (pneumonia). The **p** is silent in each case. Words starting with **ps-** are quite common but words starting with **pt-** or **pn-** are more unusual.

Exercise 1 • •

Solve these anagram clues. Each gives you a word starting **ps-**, **pt-** or **pn-**.

1 dumpy nose (**false name**) _____ (1)

2 lamps (**a song or poem used in church**) _____ (1)

3 pass is rio (**skin disease**) _____ (1)

4 pig rat man (**Artic bird**) _____ (1)

5 am cute pin (**filled with air under pressure**) _____ (1)

6 cat is shy trip (**doctor specialising in the working of the mind**) _____ (1)

Exercise 2 • •

Use each of the words you found in Exercise 1 in a sentence of your own to show that you understand its meaning.

1 _____

_____ (2)

2 _____

_____ (2)

3 _____

_____ (2)

4 _____

_____ (2)

5 _____

_____ (2)

6 _____

_____ (2)

Words ending in -re

Some words in British English end in an **-er** sound but are spelled with **-re** (theatre, centre). Take great care with these because American English uses the **-er** spelling so it is easy to become used to seeing them 'wrong' in American films, books and other media.

Exercise 1 •

List five other words in this group. Write their meanings next to them.

1 _____ (2)

2 _____ (2)

3 _____ (2)

4 _____ (2)

5 _____ (2)

Another dictation •

See *Dictation for spelling practice* (page 15) for an explanation of how to do this.

I received a brief email from my favourite niece, Deirdre, last week. She and her resourceful friend seem to be studying eight different foreign languages between them. It means that neither has much time for leisure activities. That is a pity because they both enjoy canoeing and photography and occasional visits to a symphony concert. But they have their priorities right and their studies must come first.

_____

_____

_____

_____

_____

_____

_____

_____

_____ (5)

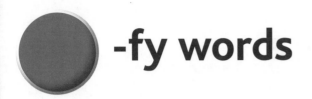

-fy words

Beautify means to make beautiful and simplify means to make simple. Quite a lot of English adjectives, nouns or even verbs can be made into verbs with the **-fy** suffix.

Exercise 1 •

Which **-fy** words mean the following? Note that the spelling of the base word sometimes changes. Use a dictionary to help you if you need to.

1 to give notice to: _____ (1)

2 to make glorious: _____ (1)

3 to fill with terror: _____ (1)

4 to make more intense: _____ (1)

5 to separate into classes: _____ (1)

6 to declare by certificate: _____ (1)

7 to put to death on a cross: _____ (1)

8 to make peaceful: _____ (1)

9 to charge with electricity: _____ (1)

10 to fill with horror: _____ (1)

Exercise 2 •

Explain what these words mean.

1 putrify: _____ (2)

2 sanctify: _____ (2)

3 testify: _____ (2)

4 solidify: _____ (2)

5 petrify: _____ (2)

6 stupify: _____ (2)

> *Some adjectives beginning with <u>p</u> take an <u>im-</u> prefix when they become antonyms or opposites. Thus: impolite, impossible, impure, improper, imperfect, impatient.*

Words with -cei-

Words such as receive and ceiling are spelled with **-cei-**. The oral sound of -cei- here is 'see'. Remember:

> Call Elizabeth Immediately.

Exercise 1 •

Choose the right **-cei-** words from the list below to fill in the gaps in these sentences.

undeceived   perceived   inconceivable   receipt   ceilinged   deceitful   misconceived

1 Get a _____ for that dress in case it doesn't fit and you have to change it. (1)

2 It is _____ to pretend that you've won a prize when you haven't. (1)

3 The almost _____ result was that our very unpromising team came first in the race. (1)

4 The _____ view of teenagers is that they are all lazy and sulky but of course that's a _____ view. (1)

5 My little brother thought there were fairies at the bottom of the garden until our cousin _____ him. (1)

6 The high _____ rooms in our house are tricky to keep clean and well decorated without long ladders. (1)

Exercise 2 •

How many words of at least four letters can you form from this word? Use each letter only once. You should be able to get at least 30.

ACHIEVEMENT

_____

_____

_____

_____

_____

_____ (30)

Word wheels

Forming words from other words – anagrams – is a good way of practising your spelling and exercising your vocabulary. Word wheels give you eight or nine letters in a circle with one letter in the centre. You have to make as many words – of, let's say, three letters or more – from those letters, always including the one in the centre. At least one of the words you find should use all the letters in the wheel.

Exercise 1 ●

How many words of at least three letters can you find in this word wheel? Each should include an **e**. Aim for at least twenty. If you find more than fourteen, you will need to continue on a separate sheet.

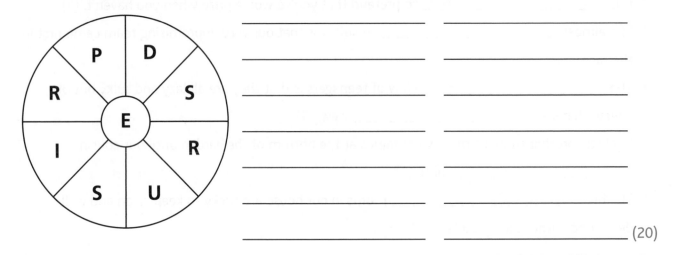

_____   _____

_____   _____

_____   _____

_____   _____

_____   _____

_____   _____

_____   _____ (20)

Exercise 2 ●

Now design a word wheel of your own containing nine letters. Start with a nine-letter word and then scramble it. Swap your work with a friend and have fun solving each other's wheels.

_____   _____

_____   _____

_____   _____

_____   _____

_____   _____

_____   _____ (20)

-ist words

A florist is someone who sells flowers (think of floral) and a dentist is someone who attends to teeth. The **-ist** ending denotes a person who does something specific.

Exercise 1

Choose the correct words from the list below to fill in the gaps in these sentences. Do the ones you know first. Then make intelligent guesses for those you don't. Finally use a dictionary to help you sort out any that are left over.

numismatist	dramatist	idealist	flautist	geologist
atheist	humorist	ventriloquist	novelist	plagiarist

1 A _____ plays the flute. (1)

2 An _____ does not believe in God. (1)

3 A _____ writes plays. (1)

4 A _____ tells a lot of jokes. (1)

5 A _____ pretends other people's writings are his or her own. (1)

6 A _____ can speak from the stomach so that his or her voice seems to be coming from a puppet. (1)

7 A _____ makes a special study of rocks. (1)

8 A _____ writes full-length works of fiction. (1)

9 An _____ has very positive ideas about life. (1)

10 A _____ collects coins. (1)

Exercise 2

Now carefully learn the spellings and meanings of the ten words in Exercise 1 and ask a friend or adult to test you. (10)

The word *facetious* (which means inappropriately amusing) is very unusual because the five vowels it contains come in the order they occur in the alphabet: a-e-i-o-u.

The silent b

Words such as lamb and tomb have a silent **b** in their spelling which just has to be learned. These words that include a silent **b** are nearly all very common everyday words. This helps because it means you are used to seeing them.

Exercise 1 ●

List as many words as you can think of that include a silent **b**.

_____

_____

_____

_____

_____

_____ (1 / word)

Exercise 2 ●

Devise a word puzzle – be as imaginative as you wish – to which the answers are words including the silent **b**. Then swap puzzles with a partner and have fun solving each other's. (1 / word)

When -ei- says 'ay'

Some words in English use **-ei-** as the sound 'ay' (eight, beige).
Try to think of these as a separate group from the ones we've
already looked at in which **-cei-** says 'see'.

> These words simply have to be learned, but fortunately there aren't too
> many of them. The commonest ones, as well as eight and beige are vein,
> rein, reign, feign, weigh, weight, freight, neighbour, veil, sheik, sleigh.

It might help you to remember that many, but not all, of these
words also have a silent **g**.

Exercise ●

Write a short poem – perhaps a limerick or haiku – which uses as many of these words as possible so
that you practise writing them correctly. If you prefer you could write a short paragraph. It can be as
silly as you like – have a bit of fun with it.

_____

_____

_____

_____

_____

_____

_____

_____

_____

_____

_____

_____

_____

_____

Mal- and ben-

Many words that begin with **mal-** (malice, maladjusted) come from the Latin word for bad. And a number of words that begin with **ben-** (benefit) come from the opposite – the Latin word for good. Remember words you've probably met in French such as *mal*, *malade* and *bien*.

In Shakespeare's play *Twelfth Night* there is a character called Malvolio (literally a wisher of bad things), who isn't very likeable. And we meet a nice young man named Benvolio (a wisher of good things) in *Romeo and Juliet*. The adjective malevolent means darkly unkind, while benevolent means kind and good.

Exercise ●

Use these words, taking care to spell them correctly, in sentences of your own to show that you know what they mean.

1 malodorous

_____

_____

_____ (2)

2 benign

_____

_____

_____ (2)

3 benefactor

_____

_____

_____ (2)

4 malady

_____

_____

_____ (2)

5 malnutrition

_____

_____

_____ (2)

6 malign

_____

_____

_____ (2)

7 beneficial

_____

_____

_____ (2)

8 benison

_____

_____

_____ (2)

9 malaise

_____

_____

_____ (2)

10 malefactor

_____

_____

_____ (2)

-er or -or?

We often attach an -er or -or suffix to a base word to indicate a doer of something: a traitor behaves disloyally; a jeweller sells watches, rings and necklaces; a cricketer plays cricket and an author writes books.

The tricky thing is remembering which words take -er and which -or because they simply have to be learned. As with nearly all spelling and vocabulary matters, noticing spellings around you and in your reading will help. The two exercises below should focus your attention on which is which too.

Exercise 1 ●

Answer these questions.

What do we call a person:

1 who runs away from the armed forces? _____ (1)

2 who takes part in a competition? _____ (1)

3 who is a member of a jury? _____ (1)

4 who studies stars and planets? _____ (1)

5 who surveys land or buildings? _____ (1)

6 from whom we are descended? _____ (1)

7 who beats time at the front of an orchestra? _____ (1)

8 who pretends to be someone else? _____ (1)

9 who secretly takes goods into a country without paying customs duties?

   _____ (1)

10 who checks financial accounts to make sure they are true and accurate?

   _____ (1)

Exercise 2 ●

Complete these words by adding an **o** or an **a**.

1 vend_____r (1)   2 perjur_____r (1)

3 football_____r (1)   4 councill_____r (1)

5 millin_____r (1)   6 decorat_____r (1)

7 invest_____r (1)   8 chorist_____r (1)

9 pension_____r (1)   10 ambassad_____r (1)

Phobias

A person who has a phobia has very deep and irrational fear of something. For example, a claustrophobic person, also known as a claustrophobe, is phobic about enclosed spaces.

Exercise 1 •

What are the following people fearful of, or phobic about? Use a dictionary to help you with the ones you can't work out. The words you need are listed below.

crowds   heights   darkness   foreigners   anything new   open spaces   flying   spiders

1 xenophobe: _____ (1)   2 acrophobe: _____ (1)

3 arachnophobe: _____ (1)   4 neophobe: _____ (1)

5 agoraphobe: _____ (1)   6 demophobe: _____ (1)

7 scotophobe: _____ (1)   8 aerophobe: _____ (1)

Another word wheel activity • • • • • • • • • • • • • • • • •

Try your hand (and brain) at a spelling and vocabulary-enhancing word wheel.

How many words of at least three letters can you find in this word wheel? Each should include an **e**. Aim for at least ten.

_____   _____

_____   _____

_____   _____

_____   _____

_____   _____ (10)

Now design a word wheel of your own containing nine letters. Start with a nine-letter word and then scramble it. Swap your work with a friend and have fun solving each other's wheels.

_____   _____

_____   _____

_____   _____

_____   _____

_____   _____ (10)

Antonyms

Antonyms are words that mean the opposite of each other. Thus good is the antonym to bad, clean to dirty, tall to short, build to destroy, and so on.

We often form antonyms by adding a contradicting prefix:

- kind – unkind
- please – displease
- understanding – misunderstanding
- religious – irreligious
- partial – impartial

One of the most interesting things about antonyms is that because English has such a large vocabulary there are often many possible antonyms for any one word, each one giving a slightly different shade of meaning. Look at these examples:

- small: big, large, tall, huge, gigantic, vast, colossal
- mutter: shout, bellow, bawl
- sympathetic: unsympathetic, thoughtless, unkind

Exercise ●

Taking care to spell your examples correctly, list as many antonyms as you can for the following words.

1 brave (adjective): _____ (4)

2 match (as a noun meaning something that is the same as something else: 'My blue cardigan is a

   good match with my blue trousers.'): _____ (4)

3 join (as a verb): _____ (4)

4 silent (as an adjective): _____ (4)

5 patience (noun): _____ (4)

6 anxious (as an adjective): _____ (4)

Double consonants in verbs

Verbs that end in a single consonant immediately preceded by a single vowel (nod, occur) usually double the consonant when they take **-ed** or **-ing** (nodded, nodding, occurred, occurring).

Exercise 1 •

Write the **-ing** and **-ed** forms of these verbs.

1 grin	_____	_____ (2)
2 equal	_____	_____ (2)
3 admit	_____	_____ (2)
4 fulfil	_____	_____ (2)
5 whip	_____	_____ (2)
6 control	_____	_____ (2)
7 mar	_____	_____ (2)
8 quit	_____	_____ (2)
9 compel	_____	_____ (2)
10 clap	_____	_____ (2)

Exercise 2 •

Working with a partner, take it in turns to dictate this passage to each other.

'Surely you're not quitting?' said Mrs Patel, whipping out her pen and grinning as she clapped her hands to gain control of the class. 'There are compelling reasons for carrying on with the game and no one has yet admitted to me that he or she is beaten.' Well, we certainly weren't wanting to admit defeat. We wanted to fulfil Mrs Patel's expectations. So we continued.

_____

_____

_____

_____

_____

_____

_____ (2)

Easily confused endings

Many words in English end **-ary**, **-ory**, **-ery** or **-ury** and because these endings sound very similar in speech you need to pay close attention to words such as secretary, unsatisfactory, artery and treasury.

There is, unfortunately, no clear rule and these words can be nouns, adjectives or verbs.

One good way of learning them is to make lists of each group and memorise the spellings as you write them. Fewer words end **-ury** than take the other three endings.

Exercise 1 •

Fill in the table with words ending **-ary**, **-ory**, **-ery** and **-ury**.

-ary	-ory	-ery	-ury	
				(4)
				(4)
				(4)
				(4)
				(4)
				(3)
				(3)
				(3)
				(3)
				(3)

StationAry means standing still. (The traffic was stationary.) Think of station, statues, status and static. *StationEry* means traditional writing equipment. (We keep paper in several sizes in the stationery cupboard.) Think of e for envelope.

Latin roots

The Latin noun *gressus* means a step. It is the basis of English words such as progress (step in front) and digress (step away from). In English many of these words are verbs rather than nouns or they can be used as both. And, of course, they often take prefixes and suffixes when they become other parts of speech.

> There are many groups of interconnected words in English that share a common Latin root. Think about convert, advert and avert, which all come from the Latin verb *versare* (to turn), for example.

Exercise 1 •

Use these words, which come from *gressus,* in sentences of your own to show that you understand their meaning.

1 transgressions _____

_____ (2)

2 aggressive _____

_____ (2)

3 congress _____

_____ (2)

4 regressed _____

_____ (2)

5 digression _____

_____ (2)

6 progressively _____

_____ (2)

Exercise 2 •

Dormire in Latin means to sleep. How many English words can you think of, or find, which are related to it?

_____

_____ (2)

Prefixes that change their spellings

Sometimes a prefix changes its spelling just for pleasantness of sound (euphony).

> For example in+mature becomes immature and in+regular becomes irregular.

Exercise ●

Use prefixes – all euphonic alternatives to **-in** – to create the correctly spelled opposites of these words.

1 replaceable _____ (1)

2 literate _____ (1)

3 mortal _____ (1)

4 relevant _____ (1)

5 mobile _____ (1)

6 legal _____ (1)

7 pious _____ (1)

8 responsible _____ (1)

9 legible _____ (1)

10 polite _____ (1)

A *mnemonic* (the first <u>m</u> is silent) is a memory aid, such as Never Eat Shredded Wheat to help you remember the points of the compass – north, east, south, west. The word comes from the name of Mnemosyne, the Greek goddess of memory. Mnemonic is the only word in English that begins <u>mn-</u>.

More word wheels

Here's another opportunity to improve your spelling and vocabulary with word wheels.

• •

How many words of at least three letters can you find in this word wheel? Each should include an **r**. Aim for at least ten.

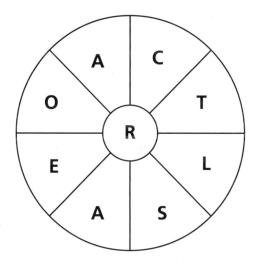

_____ _____

_____ _____

_____ _____

_____ _____

_____ _____

_____ _____

_____ _____

_____ _____ (10)

• •

Now design a word wheel of your own containing nine letters. Start with a nine-letter word and then scramble it. Swap your work with a friend and have fun solving each other's wheels

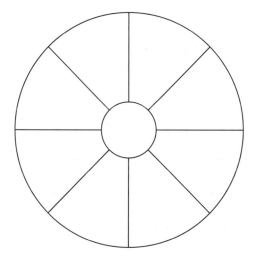

_____ _____

_____ _____

_____ _____

_____ _____

_____ _____

_____ _____

_____ _____ (10)

Words with -fer-

Another group of interconnected English words are those with **-fer**, which comes from the Latin verb *ferre*: to make or bring. Transfer means literally to bring across and defer means to postpone or make something happen later, or to yield to make yourself inferior to someone else.

When these words take **-ed** (transferred) or **-ing** (transferring) the **r** is usually doubled.

The **r** usually remains single when **-ence** is added (transference).

Exercise 1 ●

Fill in the gaps in this table. The first has been done for you.

Root word	-ed	-ing	-ence	
transfer	transferred	transferring	transference	
refer				(3)
		inferring		(3)
			conference	(3)
	deferred			(3)
prefer				(3)

Exercise 2 ●

Write a sentence that uses as many of these words as you can squeeze in, taking care to spell them properly. Don't worry about how silly and repetitive it sounds. Just have fun with it.

_____

_____

_____

_____

_____

_____

_____ (24)

Words that sometimes cause problems

Look carefully at these six words and try to learn their spellings:

separate   benefit   necessities   conceited   definite   argument

Exercise •

Now make up a paragraph of your own that uses all six words.

_____

_____

_____

_____

_____

_____

_____

_____

_____

_____

_____

_____

_____

_____

_____

_____

_____ (6)

Use this as a dictation passage. Working with a partner, each of you take turns to dictate your passage to the other, who writes it down – with all the words spelled correctly, of course! Check each other's work carefully.

> The first two consonants are doubled in *aCCoMModation*.
> And the vowels before -tion (which is the easy bit) make
> a pattern: aooa.

-duce, -pose, -struct and -clude

Here are four separate groups of interconnected words.

- Words that end in **-duce** (produce, induce, reduce, introduce) and words related to them (production, producing, induction, inducing, reduces, introduced) come from the Latin word *ducere*, meaning to lead.
- Words that end in **-pose** (suppose, transpose) and words related to them (supposed, supposition, transposing, transposition) come from the Latin verb *ponere*, meaning to put.
- Words that end in **-struct** (construct, obstruct, instruct) and words related to them (construction, constructs, obstruction, obstructs, instructed) come from the Latin verb *struere*, meaning to arrange.
- Words that end in **-clude** (include, exclude, conclude) and words related to them (inclusion, including, exclusion, excluding, concluded) come from the Latin verb *claudere*, meaning to close.

Exercise •

Write a definition for each of the following words. Try to work out the meaning for yourself using the information above. Then use a dictionary to confirm or correct your guess.

1 deduction: _____

_____

_____ (2)

2 traduce: _____

_____

_____ (2)

3 interpose: _____

_____

_____ (2)

4 depose: _____

_____

_____ (2)

5 exposure: _____

_____

_____ (2)

6 imposition: _____

_____

_____ (2)

7 misconstruction: _____

_____

_____ (2)

8 instructor: _____

_____

_____ (2)

9 excluded: _____

_____

_____ (2)

10 preclude: _____

_____

_____ (2)

Through rhymes with shoe. (I came through London.)
Though rhymes with go. (I ate it though I didn't like it.)
Think of although. *Thorough* rhymes with borough. (We gave the kitchen a thorough cleaning.)

Parliament has an unexpected <u>a</u> in the middle. If you pronounce the <u>a</u> in parliament and parliamentary you will find them easier to spell.

Homophones

Homophones are words that sound the same but which have different meanings and are spelled differently (allowed/aloud or there/they're/their).

Many of them are quite common words so it's understanding what they actually mean and seeing homophones correctly used in your reading that will help you to get them right.

Exercise •

Write one sentence for each word in the following pairs of homophones. The idea is, obviously, that you use each word correctly to discover, or remind yourself, what it means.

1 aisle/isle: _____

_____

_____

_____ (2)

2 waist/waste: _____

_____

_____

_____ (2)

3 ring/wring: _____

_____

_____

_____ (2)

4 gamble/gambol: _____

_____

_____

_____ (2)

5 coarse/course: _____

_____

_____

_____ (2)

6 profit/prophet: _____

_____

_____

_____ (2)

7 steal/steel: _____

_____

_____

_____ (2)

8 hoard/horde: _____

_____

_____

_____ (2)

9 root/route: _____

_____

_____

_____ (2)

10 yoke/yolk: _____

_____

_____

_____ (2)

Liaise (pronounced lee-aze) means to work with. 'I need to liaise with Freddy about our shared project.' Note that liaise and the related noun liaison have an extra i in the middle.

Some quirky plurals

If a word has come into English from Latin, Greek or a modern foreign language it may keep its original plural form rather than adding an **s** (or a variant of **s**), which is the usual way of forming plurals in English. The plural of formula, for example, is (from Latin) formulae. Thus you learn one formula and three formulae.

> There are also some words from other languages that we usually use in their plural form anyway. Graffiti, data and media are all plural, for example. These should always be followed by a plural verb. Thus: graffiti, data or media are/were ... (not is/was).

Exercise ●

Write the plural of these singular words. Use a dictionary if you don't know them.

1 radius _____ (1)

2 larva _____ (1)

3 cactus _____ (1)

4 crisis _____ (1)

5 criterion _____ (1)

6 oasis _____ (1)

7 fungus _____ (1)

8 memorandum _____ (1)

9 phenomenon _____ (1)

10 diagnosis _____ (1)

> *Lose* means to mislay and rhymes with snooze. (I must not lose my bus pass.) *Loose* means the opposite of tight and rhymes with juice. (My tracksuit bottoms are very loose.)

Eponyms

Laszlo Biro (1899–1985) was born in Hungary but emigrated to Argentina. There he invented the ballpoint pen and started a big company to sell them worldwide.

The Hoover company dominated the international market in vacuum cleaners for many years after the invention of the vacuum cleaner by American James Murray Spangler in 1908.

Today we often refer to any ballpoint pen as a biro or any vacuum cleaner as a hoover. We also use 'to hoover' as a verb.

Words that have passed into the language from names are called eponyms.

Exercise ●

Now use a dictionary or the internet to help you answer these questions about eponyms.

1 Who gave his name to the scale by which we measure wind speed?

_____ (2)

2 After whom are knee-length baggy knickers named?

_____ (2)

3 Who invented the system of raised dots that enables blind people to read by touch?

_____ (2)

4 Which doctor's name is given to the syndrome in which a person has delayed growth, characteristic facial features and, usually, learning difficulties?

_____ (2)

5 Who gave his name to the most poisonous substance in tobacco?

_____ (2)

6 After whom is the common snack of two slices of bread with a filling named?

_____ (2)

> *Necessary* has one c and a double s. Think of this as one collar and two sleeves if it helps you.

 # Short words for long

English is rich in synonyms – words that are similar in meaning. This is because our language is mixture of many influences (Latin, French, the Crusades, Elizabethan voyages of discovery, colonies, and so on – you've probably learned about it all in history).

And it continues. Immigrants to Britain from all over the world bring their languages with them and English gradually changes and enlarges.

Exercise •

Writers are often advised not to use a long word where a short one will do.

Provide a short word – of one syllable – that means more or less the same as the words in bold in these sentences.

1 The performance will **commence** in five minutes. _____ (1)

2 The soldier was commended for his **courageous** conduct. _____ (1)

3 Shall we **attempt** to lift that bag? _____ (1)

4 May I offer you a hot **beverage**? _____ (1)

5 I want to climb to the **summit**. _____ (1)

6 The photographer did not **perceive** the tiger until it was dangerously close.

_____ (1)

7 I need to **obtain** a new pen. _____ (1)

8 The face in that painting looks **melancholy**. _____ (1)

9 You need to **lubricate** your bike before the race. _____ (1)

10 I wonder if that castle has **apparitions**. _____ (1)

> *SepArate* (think of being ApArt). Do not confuse this with *despErate* (think of being Eager or in an Extreme position).

Does the e stay or go?

If a word ends with a silent **e** (late, prove) what happens to it when you add a suffix (lately, proving)?

There is a rule that *usually* works, although there are a few exceptions.

- If the suffix begins with a consonant such as **m**, the **e** stays (move + ment = movement).
- If the suffix begins with a vowel such as **i**, the **e** is dropped (devote + ion = devotion).

Common exceptions include truly, argument, duly, wholly, ninth, awful.

Exercise 1 ●

Apply the rule above by writing the correctly spelled words in the gaps in these sentences. The root word is given in brackets.

1 She spoke very _____. (**sincere**) (1)

2 That poor cat is _____ for its owner. (**pine**) (1)

3 I can't express my _____ for what you've done. (**admire**) (1)

4 _____ the damaged violin can be repaired. (**fortunate**) (1)

5 He _____ said nothing. (**wise**) (1)

6 I shall buy that _____ bag. (**use**) (1)

7 We shall travel _____ but meet later today. (**separate**) (1)

8 My grandparents are used to _____ with traffic noise. (**live**) (1)

9 My legs were _____ by the time I reached the finishing tape. (**ache**) (1)

10 Were you _____ speaking in front of so many people? (**nerve**) (1)

Exercise 2 ●

Write a sentence you can learn to help you remember the exceptions to the **e** + suffix rule.

_____

_____

_____ (2)

Extending your vocabulary

These words, or parts of words, come from Latin or Greek:

- **pseudo** – false (pseudonym – false name)
- **arch** – chief (archbishop – chief bishop)
- **photo** – light (photograph – image created by exposure to light)
- **omni** – all (omniscient – knowing everything)
- **auto** – self (autobiography – life story written by the subject him/herself)

Each of them is often within words in English. Being familiar with these five beginnings can help you to unravel the meanings of words that are new to you.

Exercise ●

Use these words in sentences of your own to show you understand their meaning.

1 pseudonymously

_____

_____

_____ (2)

2 pseudoscience

_____

_____

_____ (2)

3 archetype

_____

_____

_____

4 monarch

_____

_____

_____ (2)

5 photosynthesis

_____

_____

_____ (2)

6 photophobia

_____

_____

_____ (2)

7 omnipotent

_____

_____

_____ (2)

8 omnivorous

_____

_____

_____ (2)

9 automatic

_____

_____

_____ (2)

10 autonomy

_____

_____

_____ (2)

Rhythm is an unusual word because it contains no vowel. The _y_ does the vowel's job.

Words to watch

Some people like lists and learning from them. Here is a list of twenty of some of the most commonly misspelled words in English. Many of them are referred to elsewhere in the activities and tips in this book.

conscientious	immediately	argument
accommodation	loneliness	separate
necessary	occurrence	commitments
achievement	quarrelling	desperate
forgetful	benefited	potatoes
illegal	receive	definitely
foreigner	disappointed	

Exercise •

Learn the words in the list above. Memorise them by writing them down (several times if necessary), checking each time until you have the rhythm of each word and write it correctly and confidently. Get someone else to test you.

_____

_____

_____

_____

_____

_____

_____

_____

_____ (20)

And finally, now that you know how to spell these words, look up and learn the meanings of any that are new to you.